Eary
004
MAP

Let's Learn About COMPUTER SCIENCE

COMPUTERS

Jeff Mapua

Enslow Publishing
101 W. 23rd Street
Suite 240
New York, NY 10011
USA

enslow.com

WORDS TO KNOW

code Instructions for a computer in a language it understands.

data Information that is used in a computer.

desktop A computer that fits on a desk. It is meant to stay in one place.

hardware The parts of a computer that you can touch.

laptop A computer that is small and can travel from place to place.

memory The part of the computer where information is placed and stored.

microprocessor The part of the computer that handles information and completes tasks.

software The programs and other information that are used by a computer.

2

CONTENTS

There are so many things we can do on a computer!

Working with Data

A computer is a machine that works with **data**. Data can be words, numbers, videos, music, and more. People use computers at home, work, and school.

FAST FACT

One of the first computers was called an abacus. It was made of strings and beads.

Computers let us play all sorts of games.

What Computers Can Do

Computers work with data. They can solve math problems. We can use them to send email. Computers are also used to play games.

FAST FACT

The first computers were huge. Some took up an entire room!

A mouse is part of a computer's hardware.

Hardware

A computer is made of pieces that you can touch. These are called **hardware**. The pieces include the computer, screen, keyboard, and mouse.

FAST FACT

Computer parts were first invented in 1833 by a man named Charles Babbage.

Computers use software to do jobs.

Software

Computers run **software**. This is instructions for a computer. Software helps a computer do its job. Software can be computer games, computer **code**, or programs.

FAST FACT

The first software was made in 1842. It was written by a woman named Ada Lovelace.

A person works on a laptop at a café.

Types of Computers

There are different kinds of computers. **Desktops** are used at home or school. **Laptops** can be carried around. Some computers are tiny. They help run cars, airplanes, and robots.

FAST FACT

A smartphone is a computer.

**The microprocessor does
the computer's work.**

Microprocessors

Your brain can do a lot! The **microprocessor** is the "brain" of the computer. It can do math. It can search the internet. It can solve problems. It is also called the CPU (central processing unit).

FAST FACT

The first microprocessor was built in the 1970s.

A memory card stores information that the computer can use.

Memory

Your brain stores facts that you can remember later. Computers have hardware for **memory**. The computer memory stores lots of data. The data can be "remembered" quickly.

Fast Fact

Computer memory keeps your information safe while you are not using it.

Computers use electricity to run.

How Computers Work

How do computers work? They use electricity. There are tiny electric flows in a computer. They carry data. The microprocessor has parts that control the electricity.

**Your computer follows a program.
It tells the computer what to do.**

Programmers

Computers follow instructions in a special way. The instructions are called a program. They must be in a language the computer can understand. The person who writes the instructions is called a programmer.

Activity
Fun with Computers

MATERIALS
notebook
pencil
computers

Want to learn how to use computers? Here are some ways to become more familiar with them:

Find a computer. Look at home or at school. They can be desktop or laptop computers. Other computers

include smartphones, tablets, and calculators. How many did you find?

Name all of the parts of the computer that you can see. This includes the screen and mouse. Remember: there are lots of kinds of computers. Some use a mouse. Many laptops have a touchpad. Many desktop computers have a large CPU. Laptops do not.

Learn how to use a keyboard. People use keyboards to give instructions to computers. Learn where all the letters are on a keyboard so you can become faster at typing. (Check out the Learn More section for a website to help you!)

Books

Calkhoven, Laurie. *Women Who Launched the Computer Age*. New York, NY: Simon Spotlight, 2016.

Liukas, Linda. *Hello Ruby: Journey Inside the Computer*. New York, NY: Feiwel & Friends, 2017.

Oxlade, Chris. *The History of the Computer*. Chicago, IL: Heinemann-Raintree, 2018.

Websites

How to Build a Computer

www.kidscodecs.com/how-to-build-a-computer
Want to build your own computer? Use this guide to learn about all the different parts that go into making a computer with an adult's help.

Keyboard Zoo

www.abcya.com/keyboarding_practice.htm
Learn how to type in a fun and easy way. This game will teach you how to get those fingers working!

INDEX

Published in 2019 by Enslow Publishing, LLC.
101 W. 23rd Street, Suite 240, New York, NY 10011

Copyright © 2019 by Enslow Publishing, LLC.

All rights reserved.

No part of this book may be reproduced by any means without the written permission of the publisher.

Library of Congress Cataloging-in-Publication Data

Names: Mapua, Jeff, author.
Title: Computers / Jeff Mapua.
Description: New York : Enslow Publishing, 2019. | Series: Let's learn about computer science | Includes bibliographical references and index. | Audience: Grades K-4.
Identifiers: LCCN 2018001819| ISBN 9781978501782 (library bound) | ISBN 9781978502239 (pbk.) | ISBN 9781978502246 (6 pack)
Subjects: LCSH: Computers—uvenile literature.
Classification: LCC QA76.23 .M365 2019 | DDC 004—dc23
LC record available at https://lccn.loc.gov/2018001819

Printed in the United States of America

To Our Readers: We have done our best to make sure all website addresses in this book were active and appropriate when we went to press. However, the author and the publisher have no control over and assume no liability for the material available on those websites or on any websites they may link to. Any comments or suggestions can be sent by e-mail to customerservice@enslow.com.

Photos Credits: Cover, p. 1 kali9/E+/Getty Images; pp. 2, 3, 24 Best-Backgrounds/Shutterstock.com; p. 4 ESB Professional/Shutterstock.com; p. 6 OHishiapply/Shutterstock.com; p. 8 Piotr Adamowicz/Shutterstock.com; p. 10 Allmy/Shutterstock.com; p. 12 Rawpixel.com/Shutterstock.com; p. 14 jakkrit pimpru/Shutterstock.com; p. 16 Iaroslav Neliubov/Shutterstock.com; p. 18 Bacho/Shutterstock.com; p. 20 wavebreakmedia/Shutterstock.com; p. 22 Twin Design/Shutterstock.com; interior design elements (laptop) ArthurStock/Shutterstock.com, (flat screen computer) Aleksandrs Bondars/Shutterstock.com.